RINCON

WICHITA

MIG

WICHITA

WORLD *of* MADE

and UNMADE

a poem

Jane Mead

Alice James Books

FARMINGTON, MAINE

www.alicejamesbooks.org

11 10 9 8 7 6 5 4 3 2

Alice James Books are published by Alice James Poetry Cooperative, Inc., an affiliate of the University of Maine at Farmington.

Alice James Books
114 Prescott Street
Farmington, ME 04938
www.alicejamesbooks.org

Library of Congress Cataloging-in-Publication Data

Names: Mead, Jane, 1958- author.
Title: World of made and unmade / Jane Mead.
Description: Farmington, ME : Alice James Books, [2016]
Identifiers: LCCN 2016011688 (print) | LCCN 2016018430 (ebook) | ISBN
    9781938584329 (softcover : acid-free paper) | ISBN 9781938584398 (eBook)
Classification: LCC PS3563.E165 A6 2016 (print) | LCC PS3563.E165 (ebook) |
    DDC 811/.54--dc23
LC record available at https://lccn.loc.gov/2016011688

Alice James Books gratefully acknowledges support from individual donors, private foundations, the University of Maine at Farmington, and the National Endowment for the Arts.

ART WORKS.
arts.gov

Cover Art: "Our mother's house, Rincon" by Parry Mead Murray

CONTENTS

6.

7.

ACKNOWLEDGMENTS

Heartfelt thanks to Rick Barot and Carolyn Kuebler for their substantial commitment to this poem, the following sections of which appeared in *New England Review:* The third time my mother fell; Outside the window the trees; In the hills above Rincon; And when there was nothing left; We are lying in the big bed; In animal darkness, before; I bring breakfast, balancing the tray; Turns out Leo is one lying; This year I have disappeared; The hornets swarm in the diesel-filled air.; *How will you spend your courage,;* From my mother's cabin I hear them——; Mexico is a snake eating; *When this is all over;* My mother's curled up on the big bed——; In my dream my mother comes with me.; Is that MY black dog——; Just after seven we turned her; The life falls shut,; The day after my mother died; And the bit about the answer.

Immense gratitude to the Lannan Foundation for a residency during which much of this book took shape, and The MacDowell Colony for a residency during which it found its final form. To everybody at AJB, especially Carey Salerno, Alyssa Neptune, Mary Austin Speaker, and Julia Bouwsma, my great appreciation for your gracious guidance. To Gale Mead, my thanks for your sharp eyes. Tess, Kathleen, Cort, Lisa, Alan, Jeanne, Jan, Betsey, Madeleine, Andrea, Dennis, Terry, and the Horsewomen: thank you, my dear friends, for your advice and encouragement. To Ramon, Silvia, and Parry, my love.

Nancy Morgan Whitaker—

in memoriam

. . .

The third time my mother fell
she stopped saying she wanted to die.

Saying you want to die
is one thing, she pointed out,
but dying is quite another.

And then she went to bed.

. . .

Outside her window the trees
of her orchard are heavy
with their load of ripening pecans.

The shadow of the Organ Mountains
creeps across the land,
and the blue heron stands on the shore
of the shrunken Rio Grande.

Wichita, Chickasaw, Wichita, Shoshoni:
her every tree, her every row.

—Rincon, NM, July 15

...

I bring her coffee and a bun,
and a linen napkin, but—
Jesus Haploid Christ,

as her grandfather the geneticist
would say, I mean how many
linen napkins does one person need?

How many linen napkins
the size of small tablecloths
does one person need— £V𝕊

embroidered on each corner, and who
was L V S anyway?

. . .

Well, let's see, my mother begins, *LVS,*
Lilian Vaughan Sampson, would have been
your great-grandmother, the name

going back to an orphan, a boy
who took his sister's married name,
becoming Sampson in the ship's log . . .

and in this way we lost track
of that side of the family.

. . .

In the hills above Rincon
a woman is leaving jugs of fresh water
outside the Rincon Water Works

before locking the metal doors.

Rincon, where the Rio Grande
turns back on itself—
like the crook of an arm

before heading south to become
Rio Bravo del Norte. Rincon, a stop
for water on the journey north.

...

The United States of America
Does not extend refugee status

To Mexicans.

. . .

And when there was nothing left
for her to do but die,
I brought my mother home with me.

I put her in the stone cabin
by the vineyard, cabin of her X
and now dead husband, my father,

cabin he called The Fortress
in those years *his* mother
came to live there. Came to die.

. . .

With the mediocre portraits
of her three children
hung at the foot of her bed,

I tried to joke that she now
was trapped into looking
at our heads. And, trapped thusly,

she did what nobody
could have predicted:

she developed a sense of humor.
An emergency sense of humor.

That dark room in which
we finally spoke.

. . .

Remember how you wouldn't give up
your tonsils? All those years they floated
in formaldehyde? She's sitting in bed

with impeccable posture. Dots of blood
speckle the back of her cotton nightgown.
Her laugh now sounds like her mother's laugh—

a high crooning. And I'm remembering Cheracol—
the sticky bottle of red cough syrup,
my sticky hands, the swelling vapor-love of codeine,

and then my tonsils, sloughing all those years
in their baby-food jar, how I'd shake them—
my own private snow globe.

. . .

And with her impeccable posture
she kept her impeccable accounts
of life as we know it:

DATE 19 86			ITEMS	FOLIO	✓	DEBITS	CREDITS	BALANCE
1/3	86		TRACTOR OVERHAUL	CD 1		826 10		
2/28	86		TRACTOR OVERHAUL	CD 2		31 4454		
3/31	86		TRACTOR OVERHAUL			54 63		
3/28	86		BLADE	CD 3		450 —		
4/30	86		14 FOOT MOWER	CD 4		1 028 75		4904 02
12/31	86			AJE (4)			4904 02	- 0 -

. . .

We are lying in the big bed
and she says, *Are things between us good?*
—Yes Mom, things between us

are good.
Don't you think? I say.

No.

—No? You don't think things
between us are good?

No.

—No? Then tell me Mom,
tell me and we'll talk about it.

No.

—No? You won't tell me?

No.

...

Behind the filing cabinet
in my office, a mouse

begins its three-day-rot.

. . .
In animal darkness, before
the first day of harvest,
I walk up the vineyard's main avenue

thumbnail moon, and the floodlight
from the big barn. Clanks and shouts.

The squat stone structures of the homestead
vanish, its layers of ghosts flicker
and go out. The black dog Leo follows me—

almost invisible when I look back:
he floats,—a low-lying, uncomplaining
black cloud. *Day by day,* I hum—

to the dog and the moon and the vineyard,
I guess,—*Let me see you more clearly*.

Love is a ticket, whatever love is.
And to where I could not say.

. . .

I bring breakfast, balancing the tray
across the gravel to her cabin:
the evil eye. I bring fresh sheets:

the evil eye. I mortar and pestle
the methadone: *Big* Evil Eye.

I pull morphine into the syringe.

I would like a nurse, my mother says,
who can tell the difference
between a living body and a dead one.

. . .

Hospice wants to interview the patient.

But the patient says
I'm deaf and I'm blind and I'm not
answering any more questions.

(The patient exaggerates.)

. . .

Turns out Leo is one lying
thieving son-of-a-bitch pooch—

coming into my office with a spot
of paper towel stuck to his lip

just before Silvia comes in to ask
about her missing sandwich.

We take the bright spots we need,
Silvia and Leo and I.

Then the laundry room floods—
then we wring out the sheets.

...

Somewhere in New Mexico
the house that is always cracking
continues to crack.—

Somewhere in Mexico a father
pays half the ransom and gets
half his daughter's body back.

. . .

The family inundates—
The talkers talk—
The dishes crack and break—

The family inundates—

Peter has lost his darts
In the gravel by the porch—
And tied his knife to the broom handle—

The talkers talk—

My mother smiles and watches—
With those blue crystal eyes
My mother drinks it all in.

. . .

How will you spend your courage,
her life asks my life.

No courage spent of—
bloodshot/gunshot/taproot/eye.

How will you spend
your courage, how

will you spend your life.

Bloodshot, gunshot, taproot, eye—
and the mind
on its slow push through the world—

. . .

The tumor on my mother's liver
grows fast. When she lies on her back
it's as if there were a plank

and a grapefruit under the covers.
It presses on her stomach, her bladder,
her lungs. It presses on her liver,

cuts off the bile. I try to imagine.

Hospice says, basically,——
be aware:

one day she may simply explode.
Blood from her mouth and nose.

But she will not feel a thing!

. . .

My mother says
I hope we are in some proximity
to the old Palo Alto Clinic.

——Yes, I say.

But not in time.
Not in space.

...

The finest strand of deep blue yarn
connects me to my mother, spool—
unspooling.

. . .

This year I have disappeared
from the harvest routine—

the pickers throwing their trays
under the vines, grape hooks
flying, the heavy bunches flying—

pickers running to the running tractors
with trays held high above their heads
and the arc of dark fruit

falling heavily into the half-ton bins.

The hornets swarming in the diesel-filled air.

. . .

The hornets swarm in the diesel-filled air.

Wagons of grapes bump along
behind the tractor, the tractor
speeds to the concrete loading slab.

Joel backs and fills, slowly places
each bin on the truck with intense
precision—the makeshift tines

of our "forklift" slipped
onto the bucket of the backhoe.

From my mother's cabin I hear
the exhausted crews come in,
stream down the vineyard road—

their shouts distant and nearing.
And when they pass the cabin—
Viva los Estados Unidos.

. . .

How will you spend your courage,
Her life asks my life.

No courage spent of
bloodshot / gunshot / taproot / eye—

How will you make your way?

Then, *respond to the day*
some other way than blind—

. . .

From my mother's cabin I hear them—
Viva los Estados Unidos.

This year I haven't picked figs
or taken them sun-warm to the barn

or left them in the big tin bowl
where the flags of the US and Mexico
hang high in the rafters, left them

with the little sign: *Viva Mexico*—.

This year—

I haven't balanced on the wagon
picking bad fruit from the two bins,

or walked behind the pickers with my bucket,
or watched the bins being strapped
on the trucks, cinched down—

my white hands
fruit-sticky at my sides.

This year
I have disappeared.

Or I was never there.
Or I was never here.

...

Mexico is a snake eating
its tail, Mexico,—the fathers
shooting each other's sons, the sons

shooting each other's fathers, bodies
hung like flags from bridges,
as in the papers,

but not just in the papers—

home home home. The pastel
house on the river, salt cedar—
viva viva viva. Mexico

is a house on fire.

Miedo en todas partes.
Fear everywhere.

...

When this is all over
Ramon and Silvia say

we will take you to visit our home.

One day, they say, *we will take you
to Michoacán, from where we come.*

. . .

My mother's curled up on the big bed—
under the quilt like a purple sky—
big white circles for moons—.

I barely exist,
she tells me sweetly, *but you*
are not here. Then,

Shall I turn the heat down when I leave?

. . .
I want to press my body
all along her body—
hold her damp back to me.

. . .

The mouse behind the filing cabinet
isn't a mouse at all, but a rat or maybe

a chipmunk dead behind the wall—
and starting the long haul into bone-dom.

I move my papers to the dining room,
—the drafts of contracts, the permits,
—the white binder of death instructions.

The little white flags of prescriptions.

In my father's big bed
we lie face to face
and tangle our hands together.

They are almost identical
almost inseparable.

When I was young, she drew the fish
for his publications—

then he started disappearing for days
with Timothy Leary, and just like that
she stopped—and gave me her ivory ruler.

I untangle myself
and go for her morphine.

This is one of her fish:

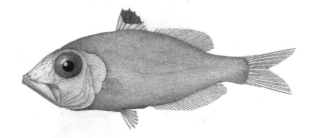

…
This is another:

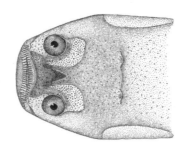

. . .

In my father's lab the aisles were narrow
the shelves were high, jars and jars:
the egg, the embryo, the adult male,

the adult female,—ocean species
of every kind staring out at us
from their sea of formaldehyde.

Octopuses and squid, my favorites—
eyes closed, eyes open, tentacles
curled out against the jar, tentacles

curled in. All that perfection.
World of made and unmade.

. . .

In my dream my mother comes with me.

We are in the meadows we call
The Flats, walking the dogs.

Walk straight past the water trough,
she says, *do not engage the moss.*

Go back to the top of the page,
the dream says, and leave out the suicides.

In my dream I walk and walk.

After a time——no mother.
After a time——no dogs.

Just the field of dry grasses
and me and the walking.

Then just the walking.

Yes dear—I would like some wine.

It's what I have to give—
dark fruit of the rocky soil.

Sorry to leave—oh, I'm really
sorry to be leaving.

Sticky tumbler, sticky straw.

—Would you like to go to sleep now?
Yes, but only temporarily.

. . .

Is that MY black dog—
with telltale compost on his nose?
Blade of grass, squash of persimmon,

some leggy insect on his forehead
next to the growth? Is that MY
red truck speeding up the vineyard's

central avenue, porta potty
bumping along behind, toilet paper
unfurling behind in celebratory loops?

...

We are sitting on the side of the bed.
What are you doing? she says—

—I'm giving you the evil eye.
You keep giving me the evil eye
and now I'm giving it back.

We laugh.

Oh. And what is this?

Those are my hands, Mom.

...

My mother takes my two hands
in her two hands and pulls herself
up to standing.

It is time, she says.

You know what to do, she says.

Do it tonight. My wishes,

while I still have wishes.

. . .

Rain, and the grape sugars
are dropping.

The phone has gone out.

...

Passing back to the house
from my mother's cabin
in the full-moon light:

her wheelchair tracks in the gravel
make a wide turn and disappear
into the shadow of the palm tree,

as narrow-gauge tracks disappear
into the deep mine shafts
of the Sierra Nevada.

In the house, the dogs
are pacing back and forth
behind the window.

. . .

At night I go for a personal best:
Law & Order: Special Victims Unit,
season 8, episodes 9-12. By day,

the grapes come in: October 10,
6 tons Zinfandel; October 16,
34 tons Cabernet; season 9

episodes 1-5. You get the picture.

My mother, in particular, would like
to get the long process of her departure
from this planet over with.

...

The finest strand of deep blue yarn—

spool unspooling.

. . .

My mother's every exhale is
somewhere between a rasp
and a scream now.

Hospice says they'll bring
phenobarbital in the morning.

Between us we have
—new bottle of morphine
—the dog's phenobarbital
—three syringes of Parry's insulin
—methadone, Haldol, etc.

Parry and I discuss combinations.
We want the best for our mother.

We do not want
to fuck this
one up.

       —October 22, +/- 2 a.m.

       . . .

       On the phone, my brother Whit
       says *Don't Google it*.

. . .

+/- 3 a.m.

Parry sits up straight, says, *but*
how can we kill our own mother?

How can we kill our own mother?

—We cannot. No.
No we cannot
kill our own mother.

. . .
So we measure the morphine carefully
with a syringe and administer it
every five minutes, as instructed,
forcing it between her gluey lips.

We no longer speak—we
no longer look at one another.

. . .
(My mother's every exhale is
somewhere between a rasp
and a scream.)

. . .

Ben! Oh, Ben,
Oh Ben, Ben
my mother cries—

anguish all over
again for the dog
with the wolf's mouth

who kept her going
as long as he
could keep going.

Then *Mitch, Mitch*
for her grandson,

Stay away from the water.

. . .

Now my mother's every exhale
is a scratchy scream.

Parry is trying to get through—
she says what it says
to say in the white binder:

Mom, let go—Mom!

But my mother's heart
is a strong heart.

. . .

I myself do what I do best:
I get under the covers with my mother
and hold a pillow over my head.

...

Just after seven we turned her
on her side to pour out
the watery phlegm—

and when we turned her over again
she had begun her dying.

...

The life falls shut,
the life falls shut
slowly. So slowly.

—Napa, CA, October 22

. . .

The day after my mother died
we finished the grape harvest
and the day after that
Ramon and Joel and Ruben

began spreading hay
on the avenues. Nobody
really spoke much.

There were little red dots
like fire, that were not fire,
on the hills across the bay.

...

She died on her 84th birthday
about which she had this to say
to herself, albeit two days early:

Happy Birthday on the very day,
and all the usual pleasantries.

...

—The never the over the void
ever the gone gone...

She always did what she wanted to do.
She ate her beans with a silver spoon.

She gave me my steely blue.

. . .

Silvia asks whether I ever feel
my mother's presence, the way we do
sometimes with the dead, who can

make themselves felt, who can feel a lot
like the speechless living when they want to,
—as when that great horned owl

stared at me from the deodar tree
while I was thinning radishes—until
I looked up and saw her glaring

and, not knowing what else to do, waved.

Truth is, I do not feel my mother's presence.
Truth is, if ever a person were to fail

to become a disembodied presence it would be

my beautiful and practical mother.

. . .

Her ashes blow off—
grit on the cold wind—
through her orchard, 2001

pecan trees, about which
she wrote me once
from what some considered

her self-exile down
by the Mexican border—
I don't know why

it gives me such pleasure
to cause 2001 living things
to thrive, but it does.

Back then, her new trees stood
just three feet high. She
pruned them standing and carried

her entire harvest around
in a briefcase, looking
for future buyers.

—Rincon, NM, November 19

. . .

Rincon, where the Rio Grande turns
back on itself before heading south
to become Rio Bravo del Norte. Rincon,

a stop on the long journey to The North—
where demand for water runs so high
that by the time it reaches Mexico

the river sometimes runs dry.

...

And the bit about the answer
blowing in the wind—
what does it mean?

As a flag blows?
A leaf downed? A leaf hanging?

Or like a piece of grit
when the last thing in the world you need
is grit in the eye?

...

Because elsewhere in this valley
working in an orchard is the man
from Mexico—who on the eve

of his daughter's quinceañera
was able to pay only half her ransom.

Can no amount of squinting bring this
into full view of the life-size heart?

. . .

In the phone photograph
of us in the orchard now,
Parry holds a tin pitcher

with our mother's ashes
and we three look small,
wizened almost, in our grief.

The trees, formidable
and orderly are losing
their leaves. The pecans

pop out of their casings—
ready for their winter harvest.

Wichita, Chickasaw, Wichita, Shoshoni:
her every tree, her every row.

Nancy Morgan Whitaker
October 22, 1929—October 22, 2013

NOTES

End Papers:
"Orchard plan" Nancy Morgan Whitaker
"My mother's orchard" Jane Mead

Body:
"account books" Nancy Morgan Whitaker (p. 10)
"fish one" Nancy Morgan Whitaker (p. 39)
"fish two" Nancy Morgan Whitaker (p. 39)

Nancy Morgan Whitaker and Douglas Hunt Whitaker on bike, circa 1934, Woods Hole, MA
   (p. 67)

RECENT TITLES FROM ALICE JAMES BOOKS

Alice James Books has been publishing poetry since 1973. The press was founded in Boston, Massachusetts as a cooperative wherein authors performed the day-to-day undertakings of the press. This collaborative element remains viable even today, as authors who publish with the press are also invited to become members of the editorial board and participate in editorial decisions at the press. The editorial board selects manuscripts for publication via the press's annual, national competition, the Alice James Award. Alice James Books seeks to support women writers and was named for Alice James, sister to William and Henry, whose extraordinary gift for writing went unrecognized during her lifetime.

Designed by Mary Austin Speaker

Printed by McNaughton & Gunn